The Dustbin Joke Book

The Dustbin Joke Book was first published in the
U.K. in 1990 by William Collins Sons & Co. Ltd.
This Armada edition published in 1991

Armada is an imprint of the
Children's Division of
HarperCollins Publishers Ltd,
8 Grafton Street, London W1X 3LA

Printed and bound in Great Britain by
William Collins Sons & Co. Ltd, Glasgow

The Dustbin Joke Book

A Load of Old Rubbish

Peter Eldin

Illustrated by Jo Wright

BEST
SELLER

What was the dustbin's ambition?
To become filthy rich.

How do you know there's an elephant in your dustbin?
You can't get the lid on.

What is full of rubbish and goes up and down?
A dustbin in a lift.

What do you call a dead dustbin?
Extinct.

What television soap was made for horses?
Neigh-bours.

What Australian animal sings a lot?
Koala Minogue.

Who delivers meals on wheels to his "Neighbours" in Australia?
Jason Dinnervan.

What did Dr Jekyll say when someone entered his laboratory?
Don't look, I'm changing.

What do you get if you pull your underpants up to your neck?
A chest of drawers.

How do you stop a herd of elephants from charging?
Take away their credit cards.

MELLY: This match won't work.

MOLLY: Why not?

MELLY: I don't know. It worked just a minute ago.

How do you measure plums?
You use a green-gauge.

Why did the two pythons get married?
They had a crush on each other.

How do snails keep their shells shiny?
They use snail varnish.

How long does a candle burn?
About a wick.

Why did the burglar rob a music shop?
He was after the lute.

Why don't snakes speak?
Because they put everything in writhing.

Where does Tarzan get his clothes?
From a jungle sale.

What game do Indian musicians play?
Haydn sikh.

What is a big game hunter?
A fan who loses his way to the football ground.

What do you get if you cross a giraffe with a hedgehog?
A long backscratcher.

What do you call a boomerang that doesn't come back?
A stick.

Why did the Red Indian call the cowboy "paleface"?
Because he had a face like a bucket.

What do fairies give their children to make them grow?
Elf-raising flour.

MRS SNODGRASS: Have you told your little boy not to imitate me?

MRS FINKELBLUM: Yes, I've told him not to act like an idiot.

What goes putt, putt, putt?
A bad golfer.

Where does King Kong sleep?
Anywhere he wants to!

JOE: What do you do for a living?

JIM: I'm a salt seller.

JOE: What a coincidence! I'm a salt seller, too!

JIM: Shake.

What do you get if you cross a complaining man with a space-ship?
A moan-rocket.

What do you get if you cross a miser with a space-ship?
A mean-rocket.

What's your husband's favourite dish?
The blonde who lives next door.

Where does a hangman buy his rope?
From the nooseagent.

What did one ear say to the other ear?
I didn't know we both lived on the same block.

The police are looking for a crook with one-eye called Scarface Mick Malone . . . I wonder what his other eye is called.

Did you hear about the man who bought a paper shop?
It blew away.

Why did the cat buy some bandages?
It wanted to be a first-aid kit.

What has five fingers and milks cows?
A farm hand.

What do you call someone who makes clothes for rabbits?
A hare-dresser.

How do you address a queen?
Tie a label to her crown.

Why did the boy put his father in the refrigerator?
He fancied an ice cold pop.

Why does a puss purr?
For a definite purr puss.

What do Scottish children like for desert?
Tartan custard.

Where can you buy British Rail bubble gum?
On a chew chew train.

What's a cat's favourite television programme?
Mews at Ten.

What is a cannibal's favourite game?
Swallow my leader.

What do you call a camel with three humps?
Humphrey.

What do martial arts experts like for lunch?
Karate chops.

What type of martial art is rather smelly?
Kung phew.

How do rabbits manage their finances?
They burrow.

What's a serious illness in China?
Kung flu.

Did you hear about the man who's invented a pill that is half glue and half aspirin?
It's to cure a splitting headache.

What's a boxer's favourite book?
A scrapbook.

What flies through the jungle squirting water at the animals?
A jumbo jet.

When is a boat like a pile of snow?
When it's adrift.

If your nose runs and your feet smell, what is wrong with you?
You're made upside-down!

Why did the gourmet climb on to the roof?
Someone told him the meal was on the house.

What did one dolphin say to the other when they collided at sea?
You did that on porpoise!

What kind of sandals do frogs wear?
Open-toad.

What do you call an old-fashioned record player?
A grandma-phone.

DOCTOR: I'm sorry to have to tell you this, Mrs Bloomingale, but you have rabies.

PATIENT: Get me a pen and paper, quick.

DOCTOR: Why? Do you want to make out your will?

PATIENT: No, I want to make a list of all the people I'm going to bite.

What snakes form part of a car?
Windscreen vipers.

Why did the idiot shoot at his clock?
He was trying to kill time.

How do fish travel to school?
By octobus.

What game is played by five elephants in a dustbin?
Squash.

What happened when the idiot had a brain transplant?
The brain rejected him.

What do you get if you cross a telephone with a flannel?
Something that is always wringing wet.

I want you to listen to my opinion for what it's worth.
OK, that means I owe you 1p.

PATIENT: Doctor, I keep thinking I'm a fly.

DOCTOR: I am not prepared to discuss your case until you come down off the ceiling.

What's white, round and tough?
An extra strong mint.

What do you call a small, laughing Indian?
Mini ha-ha.

FIRST MOTHER: What's your son going to be when he passes all his exams?

SECOND MOTHER: An old age pensioner.

SON: Dad, where are the Himalayas?

FATHER: Don't ask me, son. Your mother puts everything away in this house.

Why did the actor jump off the Empire State Building?
He wanted to be a hit on Broadway.

Why did the man drive his car into the village pond?
He wanted to dip the headlights.

ROMEO: I'm burning with desire for you.

JULIET: Don't make a fuel of yourself.

What do you call a crazy blackbird?
A raven lunatic.

What wears shoes but has no feet?
The pavement.

Why did the lazy idiot take his bicycle to bed?
He didn't want to walk in his sleep.

What tree is hairy?
A fur tree.

What magic word is used by a magician when he wants to produce a snake?
Abracadacobra.

What do you call a half-eaten apple thrown away by the Queen?
The Royal Flying Core.

TELEVISION INTERVIEWER: How can you identify a dogwood tree?

BOTANIST: By its bark.

What beans like to play hide-and-seek?
Saw-ya beans.

SON: Dad, how have you lost all your hair?

FATHER: Through worrying about losing my hair.

What lies on its back a hundred feet up in the air?
A drunk centipede.

Doctor, I have a terrible memory.
When did you first notice it?
When did I first notice what?

Why did the jockey take a saddle to bed?
In case he had night-mares.

Who is the youngest television newsreader?
The one who reads the News at Ten.

How does the musician remember his Chopin?
He always takes a Liszt.

Why did the golfer wear two jumpers?
In case he got a hole in one.

What's the most popular type of car in China?
The Rolls Rice.

What's the most popular type of car in Scandinavia?
A fiord.

What is insurance?
It is something you pay for now so you'll have nothing to worry about when you're dead!

What flies in front of your body?
A bellycopter.

Why did the germ cross the microscope?
To get to the other slide.

Some people can cook but don't.
My wife can't cook but does!

VICAR: Do you say a prayer before your meals?

BOY: There's no need, Mum is quite a good cook.

What happened to the man who bought a waterproof, shock-proof, magnetic-proof watch?
It caught fire.

Why did the lighthouse keeper and his wife get divorced?
Their marriage was on the rocks.

Why did the lamb stay quiet between lunch and tea?
He was told not to bleat between meals.

What do Australians call a tough Englishman?
A pommygranite.

Did you hear my last joke?
I certainly hope so.

First Tramp: When things get really bad there's always something you can still count on.

Second Tramp: What?

First Tramp: Your fingers.

Why don't you have an automatic dishwasher?
We don't have automatic dishes.

What's the difference between a dead bee and a sick horse?
A dead bee is a bee deceased and a sick horse is seedy beast.

What is round, bright, comes out at night and is stupid?
A fool moon.

What is a frog's favourite sweet?
A lollyhop.

What's the best thing to do when you are hungry?
Absolutely nothing – you'll soon get fed up.

Why have you got your hands in that alphabet soup?
I'm groping for words.

What happened when the idiot went to a mind-reader?
She gave him his money back.

What happened to the man who couldn't tell the difference between porridge and putty?
His windows fell out.

What has six legs and a trunk?
A fly on holiday.

Why is your language known as the mother tongue?
Because father isn't allowed much chance to use it.

Why did the ram fail his driving test?
He couldn't make a ewe turn.

What does a monster do when he hurts his toe?
He 'phones for a toe truck.

What do you get if you cross a herd of cows with a comedian?
A laughing stock.

ARCHIMEDES: Eureka!

DUSTBIN: What of?

ARCHIMEDES: Stale cabbage.

What's black and hairy and surrounded by water?
An oil wig.

Where do mules go when they are taken ill?
To horsepital.

Where do stinging insects go when they get ill?
To waspital.

Where so snakes go when they become ill?
To aspital.

POLICEMAN: Why are you driving your car in reverse?

MOTORIST: Because I know the Highway Code backwards.

MARTHA: Why has your brother got a bump on his head?

BERTHA: Someone threw a tomato at him.

MARTHA: But tomatoes are soft.

BERTHA: This one was still in the tin.

My darling, you are as pretty as a flower.
A cauliflower.

What did the orange squash say when water was poured into the glass?
I'm diluted to meet you.

What did the water say when the squash said: "I'm diluted to meet you."?
Thank you, you are very cordial.

What does a pirate's parrot have for breakfast?
Pieces of ate.

Fred and Freda are happily married.
Well . . . she's happy and he's married.

What did the police do when the perfume shop was burgled?
They put a detective on the scent.

THIN BOY: Why does everyone call you Scandinavian?

FAT BOY: Because I eat like a Norse.

When are electric weapons deadly?
When they are powered by killer watts.

What do you call a group of road menders falling down a hill?
A navvylanche.

What do you call a successful book that's been thrown in a dustbin?
A best-smeller.

Where do fleas run together?
In a flea-legged race.

DINER: The menu states that the main course is served with a choice of vegetables. What vegetables do you have?

WAITER: Cabbage.

DINER: But that's no choice.

WAITER: Yes, it is . . . take it or leave it!

BUSINESSMAN: What's the easiest way to increase the size of my bank balance?

BANK MANAGER: Look at it through a magnifying glass.

Where should you go to find a vicar?
The Bureau of Missing Persons.

Why did Mickey Mouse travel into space?
He was looking for Pluto.

What do you say to a miserable bird?
Chirrup.

Sign on park bench: Wet paint – this is not an instruction.

Why is a belt like a dustcart?
Because it goes around and gathers the waist.

Which Arab sheik invented flavoured crisps?
Sultan vinegar.

Generally speaking, politicians are generally speaking.

What live in tins discussing the good old days?
Has-beans.

Why did the miser leave everything to himself in his will?
He believed in reincarnation.

A man walked into a pet shop and said: "I'd like a parrot for my wife."

The shopkeeper said: "I'm sorry, sir. We don't make swaps."

What is never seen but often changed?
Your mind.

What happened to the dustbin when several platefuls of curry were tipped into it?
It got India-gestion.

Who brings the Christmas presents for animals?
Santa Claws.

Which animal is made of wood?
A timber wolf.

PATIENT: How long can someone live without a brain?

DOCTOR: How old are you?

What did the baby dustbin want to be when it grew up?
A big stink.

Why do you call your dog "Blacksmith"?
Because every time someone calls he makes a bolt for the door.

What do you call a fly with no wings?
A walk.

Why did the girl wear two dresses at the fancy dress party?
She went as twins.

What lives in muddy water thinking it is ill?
A hippochondriac.

Why is a cold germ stronger than a man?
Because it can bring the man to his sneeze.

At the new restaurant in town you can eat dirt cheap.
Yes, but who wants to eat dirt?

Did you hear about the idiot who was just about to step on to an escalator when he saw the sign: "Dogs must be carried on the escalator."?

He spent the next two hours searching for a dog?

How do you spell "Indian Tent" in just two letters?
TP.

What Arab with designer stubble is green?
Yasser Marrowfat.

What is brown and steaming and comes from Cowes?
The Isle of Wight ferry.

How many dustbins do you need to make a big stink?
A phew.

PRIME MINISTER: How many people work in this office?

CIVIL SERVANT: About half of them.

A dustman was walking along the road whistling and carrying ten dustbins.

A passer-by thought this was amazing and asked: "How do you do that?"

"It's easy," replied the dustman "I just purse my lips together and blow."

My friends tells me I have an infectious smile.

If that's the case, don't stand too close to me.

What is a frog's favourite flower?
A croak-us.

What does a flea do when it is angry?
It gets hopping mad.

Why did the sailor buy a pair of scales?
So he could weigh the anchor.

What do you get if you cross a dustbin with a cloud?
Something that stinks to high heaven.

What do priests do for exercise?
Hymnastics.

Why do chickens watch television?
For hentertainment.

Why are little pieces of metal good to eat?
Because they make a good staple diet.

How do you start a flea race?
One, two, flea, go.

Why did the tailor set light to all his material?
He wanted to make flares.

What gets wetter the more it dries?
A towel.

What do you call a Scotsman who makes his son polish his shoes?
McKay while the son shines.

Roses are red,
Violets are blue.
Dustbins smell,
And so do you.

Why does a baker make bread?
He likes the dough.

What has a body of metal and flies?
A dustbin.

What has four legs and flies?
A dead horse.

What else has four legs and flies?
Two pairs of trousers.

POLICE INSPECTOR: How did that criminal manage to get out of the building when you had all the exits covered?

CONSTABLE: He fooled us, sir. He escaped through an entrance.

Three drivers are queueing to go through a car wash, which one is the idiot?
The one on the motorbike!

Why does the market gardener grow crops?
He wants to earn a celery.

What is green and religious?
Lettuce pray.

TEACHER: If there were ten flies on a dustbin lid and I swatted one, how many would be left?

PUPIL: Just one – the one you swatted!

Why do dustmen never accept invitations?
Because they are refuse men.

How do fleas travel from place to place?
They itch hike.

What did one caterpillar say to the other caterpillar when they saw a butterfly?
You'll never get me up in one of those things.

What is the tastiest building in Italy?
The Leaning Tower of Pizza.

What's the tastiest tourist attraction in France?
The Trifle Tower.

Why were the two flies playing football in a saucer?
They were practising for the cup.

When do elephants speak rubbish?
When they talk mumbo-jumbo.

How can you stop a cat smelling a dustbin?
Cut off its nose.

What is bulbous, white and laughs a lot?
A tickled onion.

What's the difference between a musician and a corpse?
One composes, the other decomposes.

What is the hardest thing about learning to ice skate?
The ice.

Why did the football coach give all his team lighters?
Because they had lost all their matches.

FRED: I always put my wife under the bed at night.

NED: Why on earth do you do that?

FRED: She's a little potty.

What is red and stupid?
A blood clot.

What did the burglar give his wife for Christmas?
A stole.

What travels through time and space going "quack, quack, quack"?
Ducktor Who.

If London was flooded where would the Prime Minister live?
Ten Drowning Street.

Where would you have lunch with the Prime Minister?
Ten Dining Street.

Mother: Keep that dog out of the house, it's full of fleas.

Son: Rover, keep out of the house. It's full of fleas.

What go "squeak, squeak" when you pour milk on them?
Mice Crispies.

Boy: I'm homesick.

Mother: But this is your home.

Boy: I know, and I'm sick of it.

First Dustbin: Where do flies go in winter?

Second Dustbin: Search me!

Who performs underwater operations?
A doctorpus.

Where do swallows go?
Into the stomach.

What makes you think that your wife has better taste than you?
She chose me as her husband.

Why does a barber never shave a man with a wooden leg?
A razor is more efficient.

Mrs Snodgrass: Whenever I'm down in the dumps I get myself a new hat.

Mrs Plinge: I've often wondered where you got them from.

Mrs Snodgrass: I bought this dress for a very low price.

Mrs Plinge: You mean you got it for a ridiculous figure?

What did the boy maggot say to the girl maggot when they met in a piece of decaying meat in the dustbin?
What's a nice girl like you doing in a joint like this?

What do you call two spiders who have just got married?
Newly webs.

Customer: How much is a haircut?

Barber: Two pounds.

Customer: And how much is a shave?

Barber: One pound.

Customer: Fine, shave my head.

What do you get if you cross a dustbin with a TV?
Smellyvision.

Cookery Teacher: How do you make an apple turnover?

Student: Roll it along the floor.

What did one germ say to the other?
Don't bacilli.

What did one germ say to the other?
Keep away from me, I think I've got penicillin.

What fish are musical?
Tuna fish.

How does a farmer count his cows?
He uses a cowculator.

My wife says I'm effeminate.
Compared to her, I probably am.

How would you describe a robbery at a fish shop?
A smash and crab raid.

How would you describe a burglary at a music shop?
Robbery with violins.

What is small, pink and wrinkled and belongs to Grandfather?
Grandmother.

I used to be a fortune teller, but I gave it up.
I couldn't see any future in it.

What happened when a fight broke out in the fish and chip shop?

A lot of fish got battered.

NICHOLAS: You'd make a perfect . . .

NICHOLA: A perfect what?

NICHOLAS: . . . stranger.

How does a bird land in an emergency?
It uses a sparrowchute.

BABY DUSTBIN: Mum, can I have a chemistry set for my birthday?

MOTHER DUSTBIN: No, you can't. You'll stink the place out.

How can you make a clean sweep?
Give him a wash.

How would a bird describe its nest?
Home tweet home.

Can you describe a map of the desert in one word?
Sandpaper.

My mother is such a bad cook that pygmies come from Africa to dip their poison arrows in our dustbin.

What do you call a dancing fly?
A jitterbug.

What do you call someone who doesn't like Italian food?
Antipasta.

Why are you banging your head against that brick wall?
Because it is so pleasant when I stop.

What's bacteria?
The back door to a cafeteria.

What is brown and sounds like a bell?
Dung!

Why did the wagon train stop on the prairie?
It had Injun trouble.

Which government department specializes in deterrent soup?
The Minestrone of Defence.

DES: I do wish you wouldn't keep telling people that I'm an idiot.

LES: I'm sorry, I didn't know it was a secret.

TERRIER: Woof, woof.

POODLE: Miaow.

TERRIER: What do you mean, miaow?

POODLE: I'm learning a foreign language.

STEWARD: I've put all your clothes in that cupboard with the glass window.

SHIP'S CAPTAIN: Idiot! That's the porthole!

FRED: You are good for people's health.

NED: What makes you say that?

FRED: When people see you coming they take a walk.

NICK: I can lift a full dustbin with one hand.

DICK: That's impossible!

NICK: No it's not. You find a dustbin with one hand and I'll lift it for you.

How would you know that your dustbin was full of toadstools?
There wouldn't be mushroom inside.

How do you confuse an idiot?
Show him two spades and ask him to take his pick.

What did the surgeon say when he cut through an artery?
Aorta know better.

How do you know when you are getting old?
When the candles cost more than the cake.

MR SMITH: It's a long time since we last met. Are you still working for the same people?

MR JONES: Yes . . . the wife and kids.

Garry: If frozen water is iced water, what is frozen ink?

Larry: Iced ink.

Garry: Phew! You certainly do!

Doctor, doctor, I keep thinking I'm a dustbin.
Well, just open your mouth – I want to empty my waste paper basket.

What is pollution?
The contamination of Mother Nature by human nature.

What years are good for frogs?
Leap years.

First Dustbin: What's that funny smell?

Second Dustbin: Well, it's not me – I was emptied this morning.

What do you give a sick elephant?
Plenty of room.

HOLIDAYMAKER: Can you give me a room and a bath?

HOTEL CLERK: I can give you a room but you'll have to bath yourself.

Why did the businessman take a clock into the bank?
He wanted to save time.

Why did the finger kiss the thumb?
They were in glove.

What would you get if you crossed a flea with a rabbit?
Bugs Bunny.

How is a refuse collector trained?
He isn't. He just picks it up as he goes along.

If I killed my mother and my father what would I be?
An orphan.

Two tramps were rummaging through a dustbin when one of them found an apple.

"I wouldn't eat that," said the other tramp "There's a maggot in it."

"That's alright," said the first tramp. "There's a lot worse than finding a maggot in an apple."

"What's worse than finding a maggot in an apple?" asked the second tramp.

"Finding half a maggot," replied the first.

Gardener: I always put manure on my strawberries.

Gourmet: Really? I always put cream on mine.

What do cats try to achieve?
Purrfection.

A man asked his fiancée what she would like for a birthday present.

She said: "I'd like something with lots of diamonds in it."

He bought her a pack of cards!

How do you confuse a stupid eskimo?
Tell him to stand in a corner of his igloo.

What sea creature is good at arithmetic?
An octoplus.

TEACHER: What is half of eight?

PUPIL: Up and down or across?

TEACHER: What do you mean, up and down or across?

PUPIL: Well, up and down half of eight is three but across it's nought.

What do you call an obsolete robot?
Scrap.

Why are you scratching yourself?
Because no-one else knows where I itch.

Did you hear about the idiot shoplifter?
He stole a free sample.

What did one eye say to the other?
Between you and me there's something that smells.

What nationality is a happy dustbin?
American (A-merry-can).

What's the best way to become a puppeteer?
Pull a few strings.

What do you call the little white things in your head that bite?
Teeth.

What do bees say in the summer?
Swarm, isn't it?

How did the human cannonball lose his job?
He got fired.

Why did the human cannonball lose his job?
He was not of the right calibre.

It has a head and a tail but it does not have a body. What is it?
A coin.

I used to make doughnuts but I gave it up.
I got tired of the hole business.

"Dad, my friend Stephen said you weren't fit to live in a dustbin."

"And what did you say to that, son?"

"I stuck up for you, Dad. I told him that you were definitely fit to live in a dustbin."

What did one archaeologist say to the other?
Let's talk about old times.

GERTIE: How did you manage to break your toe?

BERTIE: See that dustbin?

GERTIE: Yes.

BERTIE: Well, I didn't.

WIFE: It says in the newspaper that most accidents happen in the kitchen.

HUSBAND: I know, I have to eat them all.

FIRST DUSTMAN: When I was on holiday in Africa last year I saw a man-eating lion.

SECOND DUSTMAN: That's nothing. When I was in Skegness I saw a man eating fish.

Our school canteen must be very clean.
Everything tastes of soap.

What's the best way to lick pollution?
Put your tongue out.

People who throw litter in the streets should be fined.
That's right. They should be taught that grime doesn't pay.

People like me don't grow on trees.
No, they usually swing from them.

What starts with T, ends with T, and is full of T?
A teapot.

What's the difference between a dustbin and a television?
You put rubbish in a dustbin but you get rubbish out of a television.

What musical instrument was invented by the Ancient Britons?
The Anglo Saxonphone.

How do you make an idiot laugh on a Wednesday?
Tell him a joke on Monday.

What's the most famous unmarried woman in America?
Miss Souri.

Who's the most famous married woman in America?
Mrs Sippi.

How do you keep flies away from your dustbin?
Put a bucket of manure in your kitchen.

What do you get if you cross a horse with a dustbin?
Whinny the Pooh.

John: When you go to the zoo you'd better buy two tickets.

Don: Why?

John: One to get in and one to get out again.

What did one garden say to the other garden?
Take me to your weeder.

Water pollution is really bad these days.
If you drown in a river the doctors will say you died of sewercide.

The British government has just come up with a marvellous scheme for reducing unemployment.

They are going to raise the school-leaving age to 65!

What did one unsuccessful magazine say to the other unsuccessful magazine?
Take me to your reader.

DONALD: I had an argument with my wife on Saturday. I wanted to go to the football and she wanted to go to the ballet.

WILFRED: Really? And what was the ballet like?

Where do rabbits go after they get married?
On bunny-moon.

How would you catch a flea?
Start from scratch.

Where do comedians go after they get married?
On funny-moon.

What did the cowboy say when his puppy died?
Dog-gone.

What did one flea say to the other flea?
Shall we walk or take a dog?

Son: Dad, I think you need glasses to read the paper.

Father: What makes you think that?

Son: There's newsprint on the end of your nose.

My mum's cooking is out of this world.
The family wish it was out of their stomachs.

Why did the mechanic sleep under the car?
He wanted to get up oily in the morning.

What do you call crazy fleas?
Loony ticks.

How do Red Indians send secret messages?
They use smokeless fuel.

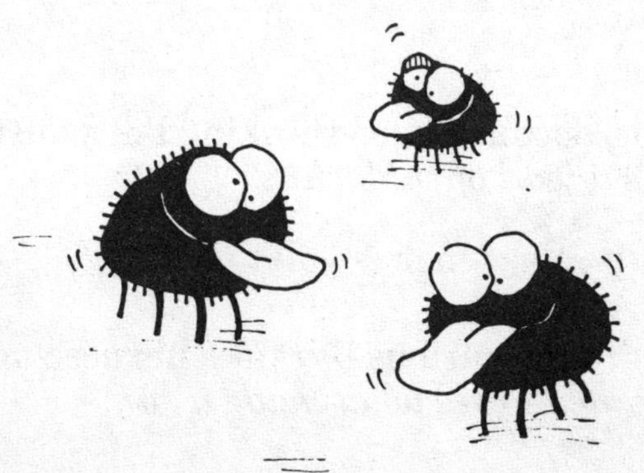

Why do some women put their hair in rollers before they go to bed?
So they will wake curly in the morning.

What's the best way to catch a squirrel.
Climb up a tree and act like a nut.

What do you get if you cross a dustbin with a silent owl?
A receptacle that smells but doesn't give a hoot.

Doctor, doctor, I keep thinking I'm a dustcart.
That's a load of rubbish!

Why did the curious boy take his nose apart?
He wanted to see what made it run.

When is a car driver like a magician?
Whe he turns into a lay-by.

What do you call an Irish spider?
Paddy Longlegs.

Why are elephants wrinkled?
Because they eat lots of prunes.

Why are guitar players courageous?
Because they need a lot of pluck.

What do you get if you cross a dustbin with a boomerang?
A smell that you cannot get rid of.

What is a forum?
Two-um plus two-um.

Why are elephants wrinkled?
Have you ever tried ironing one?

MOTHER: You're pretty dirty!

SON: I'm even prettier when I'm clean.

What's the difference between a wolf and a flea?
One howls on the prairie, the other prowls on the hairy.

First Dustbin: Why are the flies so thick around here?

Second Dustbin: Because the brainy ones are on holiday.

First Dustbin: Goodness, the flies are thick around here.

Second Dustbin: Do you prefer them thin, then?

Who is the gourmet's favourite artist?
Bottijelli.

What is an eskimo's favourite artist?
Bottichilly.

What is a desert?
An area badly in need of a flood transfusion.

First Fly: I've no idea what to get my wife for Christmas.

Second Fly: I've bought mine three pairs of slippers.

Husband: I don't know why you are complaining. I always take you out to the best restaurants.

Wife: Yes, but you never take me in.

How can you prevent a cold in your nose from going down to your chest?
Tie a knot in your neck.

Where would two motorists have a fight?
On a duel-carriageway.

Where would two farmers have a fight?
On a duel-cabbageway.

A woman went into a shop with bandages over both her ears.

"Whatever happened to you?" asked the shopkeeper.

"I was doing my ironing yesterday when the telephone rang," said the woman. "And I put the iron to my ear by mistake."

"How terrible," said the shopkeeper, "but what happened to your other ear?"

"Well, I put the iron down and then the telephone rang again . . ."

How do fishermen make their nets?
They take lots of holes and join them together with string.

Did you know that deep breathing kills germs?
Yes, but how do you get them to breathe deeply?

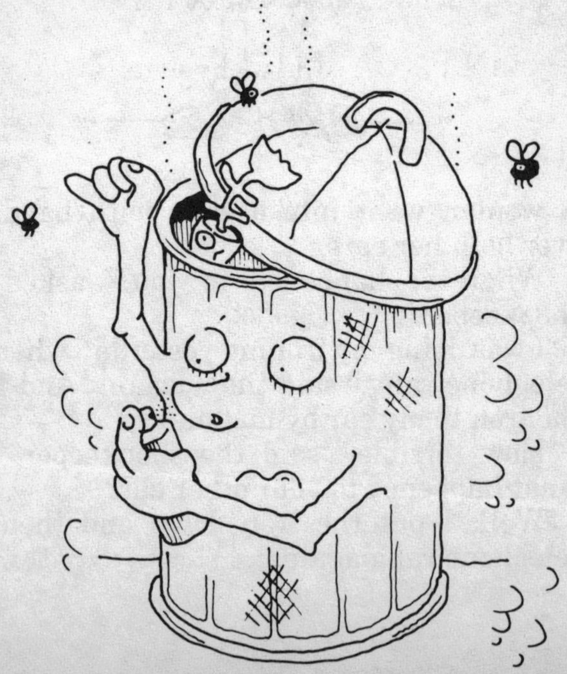

How would you describe a guillotine?
A pain in the neck.

What do you call a skinny Comanche?
A Red Thindian.

First Dustbin: Is that coffee I smell?

Second Dustbin: It is and you do.

Alec: Did you hear what happened to the flea circus?

Alex: No, what happened?

Alec: A dog walked in one day and stole the show.

What smells horrible and shoots the enemy?
A septic tank.

Which monarch is big, hairy and smells?
King Pong.

The height of bad manners is to go into an antiques shop and say: "What's new?"

What did the cobbler say when a swarm of flies entered his shop?
Shoo!

Mum's cooking is so bad our dustbin has developed ulcers.

My sister is so ugly, when a flea bites her it shuts its eyes.

What's the definition of a nudist?
Someone who wears a one button suit.

What do you call quiet shellfish soup?
Clam chowder.

WIFE: Will you still love me when I'm old and ugly?

HUSBAND: Of course I do!

The school concert starts at eight sharp. It ends at ten dull.

SCHOOL INSPECTOR: Do you believe in hitting children?

TEACHER: Only in self-defence.

Why did the refuse collector take early retirement?
He discovered that grime doesn't pay.

Why did the idiot bury his car battery?
The garage mechanic told him it was dead.

What has eight arms and tells the time?
A clocktopus.

What is air sickness?
Something that makes you look like your passport photo.

Two flies were sitting on Robinson Crusoe's head.

As one flew off he called to the other: "Cheerio, I'll see you on Friday."

What do detectives use to hang up their washing?
Clues pegs.

Where do dogs keep their money?
Barklays Banks.

What's the difference between a dustbin and a fly?
A dustbin can have flies but a fly can't have dustbins.

My brother has a mind of his own.
No-one else wants it.

What did one bluebottle say to the other bluebottle?
I must fly. I'll give you a buzz later.

I think my sister's new boyfriend is a refuse collector.
He has a certain air about him.

How do you prevent diseases caused by biting insects?
Don't bite any.

Who marched ten thousand pigs to the top of the hill and then marched them down again?
The Grand Old Duke of Pork.

What is a duck's favourite dance?
The quackstep.

What did the policeman say to the flea?
Go on, hop it.

What did the bull say to the cow?
When I fall in love it will be for heifer.

Why did the ant elope?
No-one gnu.

What did the male fly say when he saw a glamorous female fly?
What a lovely pair of legs, pair of legs, pair of legs.

How would you describe a fight between an Englishman and a Japanese?
Punch and judo.

How do you make a firelighter?
Take out some of the coal.

What is yellow and stupid?
Thick custard.

Why did the major climb a ladder at the banquet?
He was approaching the high point of his speech.

How do people in Wales eat cheese?
Caerphilly.

Why did the idiot want to buy a sea-horse?
He wanted to play water polo.

An absent-minded professor went into his local chemist's shop and said: "I'd like some prepared acetyl-salicylic acid, please."

"Do you mean aspirin?" the pharamacist asked.

"Yes," replied the professor, "I can never remember its name."

Who cracks jokes about knitting?
A nitwit.

Who likes telling jokes but never finishes any of them?
A half-wit.

96

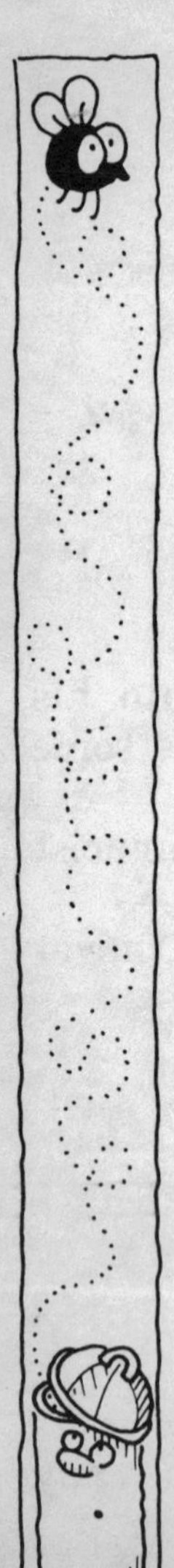

Bye!!

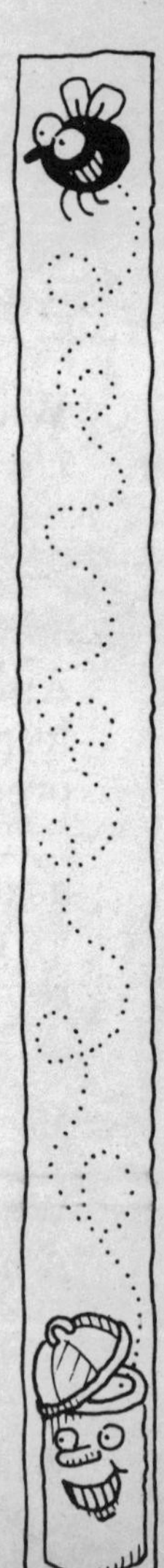